COMMON CORE
MIDDLE SCHOOL WORKBOOK
GRADE 7

Common Core Middle School Workbook Grade 7

First Edition - 03/30/15

Andrew Frinkle © Copyright 2015

TABLE OF CONTENTS:

READING: LITERATURE

READING: LITERATURE

Key Ideas and Details:

CCSS.ELA-LITERACY.RL.7.1

Cite several pieces of textual evidence to support analysis of what the text says explicitly as well as inferences drawn from the text.

CCSS.ELA-LITERACY.RL.7.2

Determine a theme or central idea of a text and analyze its development over the course of the text; provide an objective summary of the text.

CCSS.ELA-LITERACY.RL.7.3

Analyze how particular elements of a story or drama interact (e.g., how setting shapes the characters or plot).

Craft and Structure:

CCSS.ELA-LITERACY.RL.7.4

Determine the meaning of words and phrases as they are used in a text, including figurative and connotative meanings; analyze the impact of rhymes and other repetitions of sounds (e.g., alliteration) on a specific verse or stanza of a poem or section of a story or drama.

CCSS.ELA-LITERACY.RL.7.5

Analyze how a drama's or poem's form or structure (e.g., soliloquy, sonnet) contributes to its meaning

CCSS.ELA-LITERACY.RL.7.6

Analyze how an author develops and contrasts the points of view of different characters or narrators in a text.

GRADE 7 STANDARDS

READING: LITERATURE

Integration of Knowledge and Ideas:

CCSS.ELA-LITERACY.RL.7.7

Compare and contrast a written story, drama, or poem to its audio, filmed, staged, or multimedia version, analyzing the effects of techniques unique to each medium (e.g., lighting, sound, color, or camera focus and angles in a film).

CCSS.ELA-LITERACY.RL.7.8

(RL.7.8 not applicable to literature)

CCSS.ELA-LITERACY.RL.7.9

Compare and contrast a fictional portrayal of a time, place, or character and a historical account of the same period as a means of understanding how authors of fiction use or alter history.

Range of Reading and Level of Text Complexity:

CCSS.ELA-LITERACY.RL.7.10
By the end of the year, read and comprehend literature, including stories, dramas, and poems, in the grades 6-8 text complexity band proficiently, with scaffolding as needed at the high end of the range.

GRADE 7 WORKSHEETS: RL.7.1

NAME:

SCORE:

SOURCE:

INFERENCE/ANALYSIS: _____

_____

TEXT EVIDENCE: _____

_____

TEXT EVIDENCE: _____

_____

INFERENCE/ANALYSIS: _____

_____

TEXT EVIDENCE: _____

_____

TEXT EVIDENCE: _____

_____

RL.7.1: Cite several pieces of textual evidence to support analysis of what the text says explicitly as well as inferences drawn from the text.

GRADE 7 WORKSHEETS: RL.7.2

NAME: SCORE:

SOURCE:

THEME: _____

_____

HOW DOES THE THEME DEVELOP THROUGH THE TEXT? _____

_____

_____

_____

_____

SUMMARY: _____

_____

_____

_____

RL.7.2: Determine a theme or central idea of a text and analyze its development over the course of the text; provide an objective summary of the text.

GRADE 7 WORKSHEETS: RL.7.3

NAME:

SCORE:

SOURCE:

SETTING: _____

_____

CHARACTER(S): _____

_____

PLOT EVENTS: _____

_____

HOW ARE THE STORY ELEMENTS INTERRELATED? _____

_____

_____

_____

RL.7.3: Analyze how particular elements of a story or drama interact (e.g., how setting shapes the characters or plot).

GRADE 7 WORKSHEETS: RL.7.4

NAME:

SCORE:

SOURCE:

WORD:		MEANING:
#1	=	
#2	=	
#3	=	
#4	=	
#5	=	

WHAT IMPACT DO THESE WORDS/PHRASES HAVE ON THE TEXT?

RL.7.4: *Determine the meaning of words and phrases as they are used in a text, including figurative and connotative meanings; analyze the impact of rhymes and other repetitions of sounds (e.g., alliteration) on a specific verse or stanza of a poem or section of a story or drama.*

NAME:

SCORE:

SOURCE:

MEANING: _____

_____

_____

DESCRIBE THE STRUCTURE OR FORM OF THE TEXT: _____

_____

_____

_____

_____

HOW DOES THIS STRUCTURE CONTRIBUTE TO THE MEANING?
_____

_____

_____

_____

RL.7.5: *Analyze how a drama's or poem's form or structure (e.g., soliloquy, sonnet) contributes to its meaning*

GRADE 7 WORKSHEETS: RL.7.6

NAME:

SCORE:

SOURCE:

NARRATOR/SPEAKER OF TEXT:

POINT OF VIEW EXAMPLES:

_____

_____

NARRATOR/SPEAKER OF TEXT:

POINT OF VIEW EXAMPLES:

_____

_____

HOW ARE THE POINTS OF VIEW DIFFERENT? _____

_____

_____

RL.7.6: Analyze how an author develops and contrasts the points of view of different characters or narrators in a text.

GRADE 7 WORKSHEETS: RL.7.7

NAME:

SCORE:

SOURCE 1:

SOURCE 2:

HOW ARE THE VERSIONS THE SAME?

_____

_____

_____

_____

_____

HOW ARE THE VERSIONS DIFFERENT?

_____

_____

_____

_____

_____

WHAT ARE THE BENEFITS OF EACH VERSION?

_____

_____

_____

RL.7.7: _Compare and contrast a written story, drama, or poem to its audio, filmed, staged, or multimedia version, analyzing the effects of techniques unique to each medium (e.g., lighting, sound, color, or camera focus and angles in a film)._

GRADE 7 WORKSHEETS: RL.7.9

NAME:

SCORE:

SOURCE 1:

SOURCE 2:

HOW ARE THE THEMES SIMILAR?

_____

_____

_____

_____

_____

_____

HOW ARE THE THEMES DIFFERENT?

_____

_____

_____

_____

_____

_____

HOW DID THE AUTHOR CHANGE OR ADAPT THE HISTORY OF THE SITUATION?

_____

_____

RL.7.9: _Compare and contrast a fictional portrayal of a time, place, or character and a historical account of the same period as a means of understanding how authors of fiction use or alter history._

GRADE 7 WORKSHEETS: RL.7.10

NAME:

SCORE:

STORY: **GENRE:**

#1 _____   _____

STORY: **GENRE:**

#2 _____   _____

STORY: **GENRE:**

#3 _____   _____

STORY: **GENRE:**

#4 _____   _____

STORY: **GENRE:**

#5 _____   _____

STORY: **GENRE:**

#6 _____   _____

STORY: **GENRE:**

#7 _____   _____

RL.7.10: By the end of the year, read and comprehend literature, including stories, dramas, and poems, in the grades 6-8 text complexity band proficiently, with scaffolding as needed at the high end of the range.

READING: INFORMATIONAL TEXT

GRADE 7 STANDARDS

READING: INFORMATIONAL TEXT

Key Ideas and Details:

CCSS.ELA-LITERACY.RI.7.1

Cite several pieces of textual evidence to support analysis of what the text says explicitly as well as inferences drawn from the text.

CCSS.ELA-LITERACY.RI.7.2

Determine two or more central ideas in a text and analyze their development over the course of the text; provide an objective summary of the text.

CCSS.ELA-LITERACY.RI.7.3

Analyze the interactions between individuals, events, and ideas in a text (e.g., how ideas influence individuals or events, or how individuals influence ideas or events).

Craft and Structure:

CCSS.ELA-LITERACY.RI.7.4

Determine the meaning of words and phrases as they are used in a text, including figurative, connotative, and technical meanings; analyze the impact of a specific word choice on meaning and tone.

CCSS.ELA-LITERACY.RI.7.5

Analyze the structure an author uses to organize a text, including how the major sections contribute to the whole and to the development of the ideas.

CCSS.ELA-LITERACY.RI.7.6

Determine an author's point of view or purpose in a text and analyze how the author distinguishes his or her position from that of others.

READING: INFORMATIONAL TEXT

Integration of Knowledge and Ideas:

CCSS.ELA-LITERACY.RI.7.7

Compare and contrast a text to an audio, video, or multimedia version of the text, analyzing each medium's portrayal of the subject (e.g., how the delivery of a speech affects the impact of the words).

CCSS.ELA-LITERACY.RI.7.8

Trace and evaluate the argument and specific claims in a text, assessing whether the reasoning is sound and the evidence is relevant and sufficient to support the claims.

CCSS.ELA-LITERACY.RI.7.9

Analyze how two or more authors writing about the same topic shape their presentations of key information by emphasizing different evidence or advancing different interpretations of facts.

Range of Reading and Level of Text Complexity:

CCSS.ELA-LITERACY.RI.7.10

By the end of the year, read and comprehend literary nonfiction in the grades 6-8 text complexity band proficiently, with scaffolding as needed at the high end of the range.

GRADE 7 WORKSHEETS: RI.7.1

NAME: SCORE:

SOURCE:

INFERENCE/ANALYSIS: _____

_____

TEXT EVIDENCE: _____

_____

TEXT EVIDENCE: _____

_____

INFERENCE/ANALYSIS: _____

_____

TEXT EVIDENCE: _____

_____

TEXT EVIDENCE: _____

_____

RI.7.1: Cite several pieces of textual evidence to support analysis of what the text says explicitly as well as inferences drawn from the text.

GRADE 7 WORKSHEETS: RI.7.2

NAME:

SCORE:

SOURCE:

CENTRAL IDEA: _____

_____

HOW DOES THIS IDEA DEVELOP? _____

_____

CENTRAL IDEA: _____

_____

HOW DOES THIS IDEA DEVELOP? _____

_____

SUMMARY: _____

_____

_____

RI.7.2: Determine two or more central ideas in a text and analyze their development over the course of the text; provide an objective summary of the text.

NAME:

SCORE:

SOURCE:

SETTING: _____

_____

CHARACTER(S): _____

_____

EVENTS/IDEAS: _____

_____

HOW DO THE STORY ELEMENTS INFLUENCE EACH OTHER? _____

_____

_____

_____

RI.7.3: *Analyze the interactions between individuals, events, and ideas in a text (e.g., how ideas influence individuals or events, or how individuals influence ideas or events).*

NAME:

SCORE:

SOURCE:

WORD:		MEANING:
#1	=	
#2	=	
#3	=	
#4	=	
#5	=	

HOW DO THESE PARTICULAR WORDS AFFECT THE TONE AND MEANING OF THE TEXT?

_____

_____

_____

RI.7.4: Determine the meaning of words and phrases as they are used in a text, including figurative, connotative, and technical meanings; analyze the impact of a specific word choice on meaning and tone.

GRADE 7 WORKSHEETS: RI.7.5

NAME:

SCORE:

SOURCE:

HOW IS THE TEXT STRUCTURED?

HOW DO THE PIECES FIT IN THE OVERALL TEXT?

HOW DOES THE STRUCTURE HELP CONVEY MEANING AND FIT THE THEME?

RI.7.5: Analyze the structure an author uses to organize a text, including how the major sections contribute to the whole and to the development of the ideas.

GRADE 7 WORKSHEETS: RI.7.6

NAME:

SCORE:

SOURCE:

POINT OF VIEW OR PURPOSE:

EXAMPLES:

#1 _____

#2 _____

#3 _____

#4 _____

#5 _____

HOW IS THE AUTHOR'S POINT DIFFERENT FROM OTHERS'? _____

_____

_____

RI.7.6: Determine an author's point of view or purpose in a text and analyze how the author distinguishes his or her position from that of others.

GRADE 7 WORKSHEETS: RI.7.7

NAME:

SCORE:

TOPIC:

SOURCE 1:

SOURCE 2:

HOW ARE THE TWO SIMILAR?

_____

_____

_____

_____

_____

HOW ARE THE TWO DIFFERENT?

_____

_____

_____

_____

_____

WHAT WAS MOST EFFECTIVE ABOUT EACH VERSION?

_____

_____

_____

RI.7.7: Compare and contrast a text to an audio, video, or multimedia version of the text, analyzing each medium's portrayal of the subject (e.g., how the delivery of a speech affects the impact of the words).

GRADE 7 WORKSHEETS: RI.7.8

NAME:

SCORE:

SOURCE:

THEME OR IDEA:

SUPPORTED IDEAS:

_____

_____

_____

_____

_____

UNSUPPORTED IDEAS:

_____

_____

_____

_____

_____

IS THE THEME OR IDEA MOST SUPPORTED OR UNSUPPORTED BY FACTS?

_____

_____

RI.7.8: Trace and evaluate the argument and specific claims in a text, assessing whether the reasoning is sound and the evidence is relevant and sufficient to support the claims.

GRADE 7 WORKSHEETS: RI.7.9

NAME:

SCORE:

SOURCE 1:

SOURCE 2:

HOW ARE THE ACCOUNTS SIMILAR?

_____

_____

_____

_____

_____

HOW ARE THEY DIFFERENT?

_____

_____

_____

_____

_____

WHICH IDEAS/ARGUMENTS ARE USED MOST EFFECTIVELY BY EACH WRITER?

_____

_____

_____

RI.7.9: *Analyze how two or more authors writing about the same topic shape their presentations of key information by emphasizing different evidence or advancing different interpretations of facts.*

GRADE 7 WORKSHEETS: RI.7.10

NAME: _____

SCORE:

TEXT: **GENRE:**

#1 _____   _____

TEXT: **GENRE:**

#2 _____   _____

TEXT: **GENRE:**

#3 _____   _____

TEXT: **GENRE:**

#4 _____   _____

TEXT: **GENRE:**

#5 _____   _____

TEXT: **GENRE:**

#6 _____   _____

TEXT: **GENRE:**

#7 _____   _____

RI.7.10: By the end of the year, read and comprehend literary nonfiction in the grades 6-8 text complexity band proficiently, with scaffolding as needed at the high end of the range.

WRITING

WRITING

Text Types and Purposes:

CCSS.ELA-LITERACY.W.7.1

Write arguments to support claims with clear reasons and relevant evidence.

- CCSS.ELA-LITERACY.W.7.1.A

Introduce claim(s), acknowledge alternate or opposing claims, and organize the reasons and evidence logically.

- CCSS.ELA-LITERACY.W.7.1.B

Support claim(s) with logical reasoning and relevant evidence, using accurate, credible sources and demonstrating an understanding of the topic or text.

- CCSS.ELA-LITERACY.W.7.1.C

Use words, phrases, and clauses to create cohesion and clarify the relationships among claim(s), reasons, and evidence.

- CCSS.ELA-LITERACY.W.7.1.D

Establish and maintain a formal style.

- CCSS.ELA-LITERACY.W.7.1.E

Provide a concluding statement or section that follows from and supports the argument presented.

WRITING

Text Types and Purposes (continued):

CCSS.ELA-LITERACY.W.7.2

Write informative/explanatory texts to examine a topic and convey ideas, concepts, and information through the selection, organization, and analysis of relevant content.

- CCSS.ELA-LITERACY.W.7.2.A

Introduce a topic clearly, previewing what is to follow; organize ideas, concepts, and information, using strategies such as definition, classification, comparison/contrast, and cause/effect; include formatting (e.g., headings), graphics (e.g., charts, tables), and multimedia when useful to aiding comprehension.

- CCSS.ELA-LITERACY.W.7.2.B

Develop the topic with relevant facts, definitions, concrete details, quotations, or other information and examples.

- CCSS.ELA-LITERACY.W.7.2.C

Use appropriate transitions to create cohesion and clarify the relationships among ideas and concepts.

- CCSS.ELA-LITERACY.W.7.2.D

Use precise language and domain-specific vocabulary to inform about or explain the topic.

- CCSS.ELA-LITERACY.W.7.2.E

Establish and maintain a formal style.

- CCSS.ELA-LITERACY.W.7.2.F

Provide a concluding statement or section that follows from and supports the information or explanation presented.

WRITING

Text Types and Purposes (continued):

CCSS.ELA-LITERACY.W.7.3

Write narratives to develop real or imagined experiences or events using effective technique, relevant descriptive details, and well-structured event sequences.

• CCSS.ELA-LITERACY.W.7.3.A

Engage and orient the reader by establishing a context and point of view and introducing a narrator and/or characters; organize an event sequence that unfolds naturally and logically.

• CCSS.ELA-LITERACY.W.7.3.B

Use narrative techniques, such as dialogue, pacing, and description, to develop experiences, events, and/or characters.

• CCSS.ELA-LITERACY.W.7.3.C

Use a variety of transition words, phrases, and clauses to convey sequence and signal shifts from one time frame or setting to another.

• CCSS.ELA-LITERACY.W.7.3.D

Use precise words and phrases, relevant descriptive details, and sensory language to capture the action and convey experiences and events.

• CCSS.ELA-LITERACY.W.7.3.E

Provide a conclusion that follows from and reflects on the narrated experiences or events.

WRITING

Production and Distribution of Writing:

CCSS.ELA-LITERACY.W.7.4

Produce clear and coherent writing in which the development, organization, and style are appropriate to task, purpose, and audience. (Grade-specific expectations for writing types are defined in standards 1-3 above.)

CCSS.ELA-LITERACY.W.7.5

With some guidance and support from peers and adults, develop and strengthen writing as needed by planning, revising, editing, rewriting, or trying a new approach, focusing on how well purpose and audience have been addressed. (Editing for conventions should demonstrate command of Language standards 1-3 up to and including grade 7 here.)

CCSS.ELA-LITERACY.W.7.6

Use technology, including the Internet, to produce and publish writing and link to and cite sources as well as to interact and collaborate with others, including linking to and citing sources.

WRITING

Research to Build and Present Knowledge:

CCSS.ELA-LITERACY.W.7.7

Conduct short research projects to answer a question, drawing on several sources and generating additional related, focused questions for further research and investigation.

CCSS.ELA-LITERACY.W.7.8

Gather relevant information from multiple print and digital sources, using search terms effectively; assess the credibility and accuracy of each source; and quote or paraphrase the data and conclusions of others while avoiding plagiarism and following a standard format for citation.

CCSS.ELA-LITERACY.W.7.9

Draw evidence from literary or informational texts to support analysis, reflection, and research.

- CCSS.ELA-LITERACY.W.7.9.A

Apply *grade 7 Reading standards* to literature (e.g., "Compare and contrast a fictional portrayal of a time, place, or character and a historical account of the same period as a means of understanding how authors of fiction use or alter history").

- CCSS.ELA-LITERACY.W.7.9.B

Apply *grade 7 Reading standards* to literary nonfiction (e.g. "Trace and evaluate the argument and specific claims in a text, assessing whether the reasoning is sound and the evidence is relevant and sufficient to support the claims").

GRADE 7 STANDARDS

WRITING

Range of Writing:

CCSS.ELA-LITERACY.W.7.10

Write routinely over extended time frames (time for research, reflection, and revision) and shorter time frames (a single sitting or a day or two) for a range of discipline-specific tasks, purposes, and audiences.

NAME:

SCORE:

ARGUMENT FOR: _____

_____

SUPPORT: _____

_____

_____

ARGUMENT AGAINST: _____

_____

SUPPORT: _____

_____

_____

CONCLUSION: _____

_____

_____

W.7.1.A-E: Write arguments to support claims with clear reasons and relevant evidence. Introduce claim(s), acknowledge alternate or opposing claims, and organize the reasons and evidence logically. Support claim(s) with logical reasoning and relevant evidence, using accurate, credible sources and demonstrating an understanding of the topic or text. Use words, phrases, and clauses to create cohesion and clarify the relationships among claim(s), reasons, and evidence. Establish and maintain a formal style. Provide a concluding statement or section that follows from and supports the argument presented.

NAME:

SCORE:

TITLE:

TOPIC/MAIN IDEA: _____

_____

SOURCES: _____

_____

NOTES: _____

_____

_____

_____

_____

_____

_____

W.7.2.A-F: *Write informative/explanatory texts to examine a topic and convey ideas, concepts, and information through the selection, organization, and analysis of relevant content. Introduce a topic clearly, previewing what is to follow; organize ideas, concepts, and information, using strategies such as definition, classification, comparison/ contrast, and cause/effect; include formatting (e.g., headings), graphics (e.g., charts, tables), and multimedia when useful to aiding comprehension. Develop the topic with relevant facts, definitions, concrete details, quotations, or other information and examples. Use appropriate transitions to create cohesion and clarify the relationships among ideas and concepts. Use precise language and domain-specific vocabulary to inform about or explain the topic. Establish and maintain formal style. Provide a concluding statement or section that follows from and supports the information or explanation presented.*

NAME:

SCORE:

TITLE:

_____

_____

_____

_____

_____

_____

_____

_____

_____

_____

_____

*ADD GRAPHICS AND SUPPORTING MULTIMEDIA IF POSSIBLE

W.7.2.A-F: SEE PAGE 1 FOR STANDARDS AND EXPECTATIONS

NAME:

SCORE:

TITLE:

STORY TOPIC: _____

_____

CHARACTERS:

EVENT: _____

_____

EVENT: _____

_____

EVENT: _____

_____

CONCLUSION: _____

_____

W.7.3.A-E: Write narratives to develop real or imagined experiences or events using effective technique, relevant descriptive details, and well-structured event sequences. Engage and orient the reader by establishing a context and point of view and introducing a narrator and/or characters; organize an event sequence that unfolds naturally and logically. Use narrative techniques, such as dialogue, pacing, and description, to develop experiences, events, and/ or characters. Use a variety of transition words, phrases, and clauses to convey sequence and signal shifts from one time frame or setting to another. Use precise words and phrases, relevant descriptive details, and sensory language to capture the action and convey experiences and events. Provide a conclusion that follows from and reflects on the narrated experiences or events.

NAME:

SCORE:

TITLE:

_____

_____

_____

_____

_____

_____

_____

_____

_____

_____

_____

NAME:

SCORE:

TITLE:

_____

_____

_____

_____

_____

_____

_____

_____

_____

_____

_____

_____

_____

_____

_____

W.7.3.A-E: SEE PAGE 1 FOR STANDARDS AND EXPECTATIONS

GRADE 7 WORKSHEETS: W.7.4

NAME:

SCORE:

TITLE:

PURPOSE:

AUDIENCE:

_____

_____

_____

_____

_____

_____

_____

_____

_____

_____

W.7.4: _Produce clear and coherent writing in which the development, organization, and style are appropriate to task, purpose, and audience._

NAME:

SCORE:

TITLE:

ROUGH DRAFT: _____

_____

_____

_____

_____

_____

_____

_____

_____

_____

EDITED BY:

W.7.5: *With some guidance and support from peers and adults, develop and strengthen writing as needed by planning, revising, editing, rewriting, or trying a new approach, focusing on how well purpose and audience have been addressed. (Editing for conventions should demonstrate command of Language standards 1-3 up to and including grade 7).*

NAME:

SCORE:

TITLE:

FINAL DRAFT: _____

_____

_____

_____

_____

_____

_____

_____

_____

_____

_____

_____

_____

_____

NAME:

SCORE:

TOPIC:

SOURCE 1:

NOTES FROM SOURCE 1:

_____

_____

_____

SOURCE 2:

NOTES FROM SOURCE 2:

_____

_____

_____

HOW DID YOU USE TECHNOLOGY AND/OR THE INTERNET FOR WRITING?

_____

_____

W.7.6: Use technology, including the Internet, to produce and publish writing and link to and cite sources as well as to interact and collaborate with others, including linking to and citing sources.

NAME:

SCORE:

TITLE:

ROUGH DRAFT: _____

_____

_____

_____

_____

_____

_____

_____

_____

_____

_____

_____

_____

*USE YOUR NOTES AND ROUGH DRAFT TO TYPE A PAPER

W.7.6: *SEE PAGE 1 FOR STANDARDS AND EXPECTATIONS*

NAME:

SCORE:

WORKS CITED/BIBLIOGRAPHY

SOURCE:

SOURCE:

SOURCE:

SOURCE:

NAME:

SCORE:

RESEARCH QUESTION:

SOURCE 1:

NOTES FROM SOURCE 1:

SOURCE 2:

NOTES FROM SOURCE 2:

SOURCE 3:

NOTES FROM SOURCE 3:

W.7.7: *Conduct short research projects to answer a question, drawing on several sources and generating additional related, focused questions for further research and investigation.*

NAME:

SCORE:

TITLE:

RESEARCH: _____

_____

_____

_____

_____

_____

_____

_____

_____

_____

_____

_____

FOLLOW-UP RESEARCH QUESTIONS:

_____

_____

W.7.7: SEE PAGE 1 FOR STANDARDS AND EXPECTATIONS

MIDDLE SCHOOL COMMON CORE ASSESSMENTS (C) 2015 Andrew Frinkle

NAME:

SCORE:

TOPIC/QUESTION:

SOURCE 1:

NOTES FROM SOURCE 1:

SOURCE 2:

NOTES FROM SOURCE 2:

WHY ARE THESE SOURCES CREDIBLE?

W.7.8: *Gather relevant information from multiple print and digital sources, using search terms effectively; assess the credibility and accuracy of each source; and quote or paraphrase the data and conclusions of others while avoiding plagiarism and following a standard format for citation.*

NAME:

SCORE:

TITLE:

USE YOUR SOURCES IN A PAPER: _____

_____

_____

_____

_____

_____

_____

_____

_____

_____

_____

_____

_____

W.7.8: SEE PAGE 1 FOR STANDARDS AND EXPECTATIONS

NAME:

SCORE:

WORKS CITED/BIBLIOGRAPHY

SOURCE:

SOURCE:

SOURCE:

SOURCE:

GRADE 7 WORKSHEETS: W.7.9.A-B (page 1)

NAME:

SCORE:

TOPIC/RESEARCH QUESTION:

SOURCE 1:

SOURCE 2:

HOW ARE THE SOURCES SIMILAR?	HOW ARE THE SOURCES DIFFERENT?

HOW ACCURATE ARE THE SOURCES?

W.7.9.A-B: Draw evidence from literary or informational texts to support analysis, reflection, and research. Apply grade 7 Reading standards to literature (e.g., "Compare and contrast a fictional portrayal of a time, place, or character and a historical account of the same period as a means of understanding how authors of fiction use or alter history"). Apply grade 7 Reading standards to literary nonfiction (e.g. "Trace and evaluate the argument and specific claims in a text, assessing whether the reasoning is sound and the evidence is relevant and sufficient to support the claims").

NAME:

SCORE:

TITLE:

REFLECTION/RESEARCH PAPER: _____

_____

_____

_____

_____

_____

_____

_____

_____

_____

_____

_____

_____

_____

W.7.9.A-B: *SEE PAGE 1 FOR STANDARDS AND EXPECTATIONS*

NAME:

SCORE:

TITLE:	PURPOSE/GENRE:	AUDIENCE:
#1 _____	QUICK-WRITE	_____
#2 _____	QUICK-WRITE	_____
#3 _____	NARRATIVE	_____
#4 _____	INFORMATIVE	_____
#5 _____	RESEARCH	_____
#6 _____	ROUGH DRAFT	_____
#7 _____	REVISION	_____
#8 _____	_____	_____
#9 _____	_____	_____
#10 _____	_____	_____

W.7.10: *Write routinely over extended time frames (time for research, reflection, and revision) and shorter time frames (a single sitting or a day or two) for a range of discipline-specific tasks, purposes, and audiences.*

NAME:

SCORE:

GRADE 7 WORKSHEETS: BIBLIOGRAPHY

NAME:

SCORE:

WORKS CITED/BIBLIOGRAPHY

SOURCE:

SOURCE:

SOURCE:

SOURCE:

SOURCE:

GRADE 7 WORKSHEETS: WRITING LOG

NAME:

SCORE:

	TITLE:	PURPOSE/GENRE:	AUDIENCE:
#1			
#2			
#3			
#4			
#5			
#6			
#7			
#8			
#9			
#10			

SPEAKING & LISTENING

GRADE 7 STANDARDS

SPEAKING & LISTENING

Comprehension and Collaboration:

CCSS.ELA-LITERACY.SL.7.1

Engage effectively in a range of collaborative discussions (one-on-one, in groups, and teacher-led) with diverse partners on grade 7 topics, texts, and issues, building on others' ideas and expressing their own clearly.

- CCSS.ELA-LITERACY.SL.7.1.A

Come to discussions prepared, having read or researched material under study; explicitly draw on that preparation by referring to evidence on the topic, text, or issue to probe and reflect on ideas under discussion.

- CCSS.ELA-LITERACY.SL.7.1.B

Follow rules for collegial discussions, track progress toward specific goals and deadlines, and define individual roles as needed.

- CCSS.ELA-LITERACY.SL.7.1.C

Pose questions that elicit elaboration and respond to others' questions and comments with relevant observations and ideas that bring the discussion back on topic as needed.

- CCSS.ELA-LITERACY.SL.7.1.D

Acknowledge new information expressed by others and, when warranted, modify their own views.

GRADE 7 STANDARDS

SPEAKING & LISTENING

Comprehension and Collaboration (continued):

CCSS.ELA-LITERACY.SL.7.2

Analyze the main ideas and supporting details presented in diverse media and formats (e.g., visually, quantitatively, orally) and explain how the ideas clarify a topic, text, or issue under study.

CCSS.ELA-LITERACY.SL.7.3

Delineate a speaker's argument and specific claims, evaluating the soundness of the reasoning and the relevance and sufficiency of the evidence.

Presentation of Knowledge and Ideas:

CCSS.ELA-LITERACY.SL.7.4

Present claims and findings, emphasizing salient points in a focused, coherent manner with pertinent descriptions, facts, details, and examples; use appropriate eye contact, adequate volume, and clear pronunciation.

CCSS.ELA-LITERACY.SL.7.5

Include multimedia components and visual displays in presentations to clarify claims and findings and emphasize salient points.

CCSS.ELA-LITERACY.SL.7.6

Adapt speech to a variety of contexts and tasks, demonstrating command of formal English when indicated or appropriate. (See grade 7 Language standards 1 and 3 here for specific expectations.)

GRADE 7 WORKSHEETS: SL.7.1.A-D

NAME:

SCORE:

DISCUSSION TOPIC:

REFERENCES:

WHAT DID OTHERS SAY?

_____

_____

_____

_____

_____

_____

WHAT DID I CONTRIBUTE?

_____

_____

_____

_____

_____

_____

DISCUSSION SUMMARY: _____

_____

_____

SL.7.1.A-D: Engage effectively in a range of collaborative discussions (one-on-one, in groups, and teacher-led) with diverse partners on grade 7 topics, texts, and issues, building on others' ideas and expressing their own clearly. Come to discussions prepared, having read or researched material under study; explicitly draw on that preparation by referring to evidence on the topic, text, or issue to probe and reflect on ideas under discussion. Follow rules for collegial discussions, track progress toward specific goals and deadlines, and define individual roles as needed. Pose questions that elicit elaboration and respond to others' questions and comments with relevant observations and ideas that bring the discussion back on topic as needed. Acknowledge new information expressed by others and, when warranted, modify their own views.

NAME:

SCORE:

TOPIC:

SOURCE 1:

FORMAT:

MAIN IDEA(S): _____

_____

HOW DOES THE SOURCE CONTRIBUTE TO THE TOPIC? _____

_____

_____

SOURCE 2:

FORMAT:

MAIN IDEA(S): _____

_____

HOW DOES THE SOURCE CONTRIBUTE TO THE TOPIC? _____

_____

_____

SL.7.2: *Analyze the main ideas and supporting details presented in diverse media and formats (e.g., visually, quantitatively, orally) and explain how the ideas clarify a topic, text, or issue under study.*

NAME:

SCORE:

ARGUMENT:

WHICH PARTS ARE FACT-BASED?

_____

_____

_____

_____

_____

_____

WHICH PARTS ARE OPINIONS?

_____

_____

_____

_____

_____

_____

IS THE SPEAKER'S ARGUMENT MORE FACT-BASED OR OPINION-BASED? WHY?

_____

_____

_____

_____

SL.7.3: _Delineate a speaker's argument and specific claims, evaluating the soundness of the reasoning and the relevance and sufficiency of the evidence._

GRADE 7 WORKSHEETS: SL.7.4

NAME: _____

SCORE: _____

IDEA/ARGUMENT: _____

_____

_____

SUPPORTING DETAILS: _____

_____

SUPPORTING DETAILS: _____

_____

SUMMARY: _____

_____

_____

---

*PRESENT YOUR TOPIC WITH PROPER EYE CONTACT, VOLUME, & PRONUNCIATION

SL.7.4: *Present claims and findings, emphasizing salient points in a focused, coherent manner with pertinent descriptions, facts, details, and examples; use appropriate eye contact, adequate volume, and clear pronunciation.*

NAME:

SCORE:

MAIN POINTS/IDEA: _____

_____

_____

_____

_____

MULTIMEDIA SOURCE:

HOW DOES THIS SOURCE SUPPORT THE TOPIC? _____

_____

MULTIMEDIA SOURCE:

HOW DOES THIS SOURCE SUPPORT THE TOPIC? _____

_____

*PRESENT YOUR TOPIC WITH MULTIMEDIA SUPPORT

SL.7.5: Include multimedia components and visual displays in presentations to clarify claims and findings and emphasize salient points.

NAME:

SCORE:

SPEECH SITUATION: _____

_____

GIVE EXAMPLES OF HOW YOU ADAPTED YOUR SPEECH/LANGUAGE TO THE SITUATION:

_____

_____

_____

SPEECH SITUATION: _____

_____

GIVE EXAMPLES OF HOW YOU ADAPTED YOUR SPEECH/LANGUAGE TO THE SITUATION:

_____

_____

_____

SL.7.6: Adapt speech to a variety of contexts and tasks, demonstrating command of formal English when indicated or appropriate. (See grade 7 Language standards 1 and 3 here for specific expectations.)

LANGUAGE

GRADE 7 STANDARDS

LANGUAGE

Conventions of Standard English:

CCSS.ELA-LITERACY.L.7.1

Demonstrate command of the conventions of standard English grammar and usage when writing or speaking.

- CCSS.ELA-LITERACY.L.7.1.A

Explain the function of phrases and clauses in general and their function in specific sentences.

- CCSS.ELA-LITERACY.L.7.1.B

Choose among simple, compound, complex, and compound-complex sentences to signal differing relationships among ideas.

- CCSS.ELA-LITERACY.L.7.1.C

Place phrases and clauses within a sentence, recognizing and correcting misplaced and dangling modifiers.

CCSS.ELA-LITERACY.L.7.2

Demonstrate command of the conventions of standard English capitalization, punctuation, and spelling when writing.

- CCSS.ELA-LITERACY.L.7.2.A

Use a comma to separate coordinate adjectives (e.g., *It was a fascinating, enjoyable movie* but not *He wore an old[,] green shirt*).

- CCSS.ELA-LITERACY.L.7.2.B

Spell correctly.

LANGUAGE

Knowledge of Language:

CCSS.ELA-LITERACY.L.7.3

Use knowledge of language and its conventions when writing, speaking, reading, or listening.

- CCSS.ELA-LITERACY.L.7.3.A

Choose language that expresses ideas precisely and concisely, recognizing and eliminating wordiness and redundancy.

Vocabulary Acquisition and Use:

CCSS.ELA-LITERACY.L.7.4

Determine or clarify the meaning of unknown and multiple-meaning words and phrases based on *grade 7 reading and content*, choosing flexibly from a range of strategies.

- CCSS.ELA-LITERACY.L.7.4.A

Use context (e.g., the overall meaning of a sentence or paragraph; a word's position or function in a sentence) as a clue to the meaning of a word or phrase.

- CCSS.ELA-LITERACY.L.7.4.B

Use common, grade-appropriate Greek or Latin affixes and roots as clues to the meaning of a word (e.g., *belligerent, bellicose, rebel*).

- CCSS.ELA-LITERACY.L.7.4.C

Consult general and specialized reference materials (e.g., dictionaries, glossaries, thesauruses), both print and digital, to find the pronunciation of a word or determine or clarify its precise meaning or its part of speech.

- CCSS.ELA-LITERACY.L.7.4.D

Verify the preliminary determination of the meaning of a word or phrase (e.g., by checking the inferred meaning in context or in a dictionary).

LANGUAGE

Vocabulary Acquisition and Use (continued):

CCSS.ELA-LITERACY.L.7.5

Demonstrate understanding of figurative language, word relationships, and nuances in word meanings.

- CCSS.ELA-LITERACY.L.7.5.A

Interpret figures of speech (e.g., literary, biblical, and mythological allusions) in context.

- CCSS.ELA-LITERACY.L.7.5.B

Use the relationship between particular words (e.g., synonym/antonym, analogy) to better understand each of the words.

- CCSS.ELA-LITERACY.L.7.5.C

Distinguish among the connotations (associations) of words with similar denotations (definitions) (e.g., *refined, respectful, polite, diplomatic, condescending*).

CCSS.ELA-LITERACY.L.7.6

Acquire and use accurately grade-appropriate general academic and domain-specific words and phrases; gather vocabulary knowledge when considering a word or phrase important to comprehension or expression.

NAME:

SCORE:

SENTENCE:

CLAUSE/PHRASE:

USAGE:

CLAUSE/PHRASE:

USAGE:

CLAUSE/PHRASE:

USAGE:

L.7.1.A-C: Demonstrate command of the conventions of standard English grammar and usage when writing or speaking. Explain the function of phrases and clauses in general and their function in specific sentences. Choose among simple, compound, complex, and compound-complex sentences to signal differing relationships among ideas. Place phrases and clauses within a sentence, recognizing and correcting misplaced and dangling modifiers.

NAME:

SCORE:

ORIGINAL SENTENCE(S): _____

_____

_____

_____

FIX/REWRITE SENTENCE(S): _____

_____

_____

FIX/REWRITE SENTENCE(S): _____

_____

_____

FIX/REWRITE SENTENCE(S): _____

_____

_____

L.6.1.A-C: SEE PAGE 1 FOR STANDARDS AND EXPECTATIONS

NAME:

SCORE:

WRITE WITH SEVERAL EXAMPLES OF CORRECT CAPITALIZATION AND SPELLING:

_____

_____

_____

_____

_____

WRITE WITH SEVERAL EXAMPLES OF CORRECT PUNCTUATION AND SPELLING:

_____

_____

_____

_____

_____

L.6.2.A-B: *Demonstrate command of the conventions of standard English capitalization, punctuation, and spelling when writing. Use a comma to separate coordinate adjectives (e.g., It was a fascinating, enjoyable movie but not He wore an old[,] green shirt). Spell correctly.*

NAME:

SCORE:

WRITE WITH CORRECT CAPITALIZATION, PUNCTUATION, AND SPELLING:

_____

_____

_____

_____

_____

_____

_____

_____

_____

_____

_____

_____

_____

_____

L.7.2.A-C: SEE PAGE 1 FOR STANDARDS

NAME:

SCORE:

TEXT/SPEECH SAMPLE: _____

_____

_____

_____

HOW WOULD YOU SAY THIS DIFFERENTLY IF WRITING? _____

_____

_____

HOW WOULD YOU SAY THIS DIFFERENTLY IF SPEAKING? _____

_____

_____

WHAT IS ANOTHER WAY TO SAY THIS? _____

_____

_____

L.7.3: Use knowledge of language and its conventions when writing, speaking, reading, or listening. Choose language that expresses ideas precisely and concisely, recognizing and eliminating wordiness and redundancy.

NAME:

SCORE:

TEXT/SPEECH SAMPLE: _____

_____

_____

_____

_____

HOW COULD THIS SAMPLE BE IMPROVED? _____

_____

_____

REWRITE THE SAMPLE: _____

_____

_____

_____

_____

_____

L.7.3: SEE PAGE 1 FOR STANDARDS

NAME:

SCORE:

WORD:

ROOT/AFFIXES:

GUESS:

CLUES:

ACTUAL DEFINITION: _____

_____

WORD:

ROOT/AFFIXES:

GUESS:

CLUES:

ACTUAL DEFINITION: _____

_____

L.7.4.A-D: *Determine or clarify the meaning of unknown and multiple-meaning words and phrases based on grade 7 reading and content, choosing flexibly from a range of strategies. Use context (e.g., the overall meaning of a sentence or paragraph; a word's position or function in a sentence) as a clue to the meaning of a word or phrase. Use common, grade-appropriate Greek or Latin affixes and roots as clues to the meaning of a word (e.g., belligerent, bellicose, rebel). Consult general and specialized reference materials (e.g., dictionaries, glossaries, thesauruses), both print and digital, to find the pronunciation of a word or determine or clarify its precise meaning or its part of speech. Verify the preliminary determination of the meaning of a word or phrase (e.g., by checking the inferred meaning in context or in a dictionary).*

NAME:

SCORE:

WORD:

REFERENCE:

MEANING:

USE IT IN A SENTENCE:

WORD:

REFERENCE:

MEANING:

USE IT IN A SENTENCE:

WORD:

REFERENCE:

MEANING:

USE IT IN A SENTENCE:

L.7.4.A-D: *SEE PAGE 1 FOR STANDARDS AND EXPECTATIONS*

NAME:

SCORE:

WORD/PHRASE:

CLUES:

MEANING:

WORD/PHRASE:

CLUES:

MEANING:

WORD/PHRASE:

CLUES:

MEANING:

L.7.5.A-C: Demonstrate understanding of figurative language, word relationships, and nuances in word meanings. Interpret figures of speech (e.g., literary, biblical, and mythological allusions) in context. Use the relationship between particular words (e.g., synonym/antonym, analogy) to better understand each of the words. Distinguish among the connotations (associations) of words with similar denotations (definitions) (e.g., refined, respectful, polite, diplomatic, condescending).

MIDDLE SCHOOL COMMON CORE ASSESSMENTS (C) 2015 Andrew Frinkle

NAME:

SCORE:

WORD/PHRASE:

MEANING: _____

_____

CONNOTATION:

WORD/PHRASE:

MEANING: _____

_____

CONNOTATION:

WORD/PHRASE:

MEANING: _____

_____

CONNOTATION:

L.7.5.A-C: SEE PAGE 1 FOR STANDARDS AND EXPECTATIONS

NAME:

SCORE:

WORD/PHRASE:

USE IT CORRECTLY:

WORD/PHRASE:

USE IT CORRECTLY:

WORD/PHRASE:

USE IT CORRECTLY:

WORD/PHRASE:

USE IT CORRECTLY:

L.7.6: Acquire and use accurately grade-appropriate general academic and domain-specific words and phrases; gather vocabulary knowledge when considering a word or phrase important to comprehension or expression.

HISTORY &
SOCIAL STUDIES

GRADE 7 STANDARDS

HISTORY & SOCIAL STUDIES

Key Ideas and Details:

CCSS.ELA-LITERACY.RH.6-8.1

Cite specific textual evidence to support analysis of primary and secondary sources.

CCSS.ELA-LITERACY.RH.6-8.2

Determine the central ideas or information of a primary or secondary source; provide an accurate summary of the source distinct from prior knowledge or opinions.

CCSS.ELA-LITERACY.RH.6-8.3

Identify key steps in a text's description of a process related to history/social studies (e.g., how a bill becomes law, how interest rates are raised or lowered).

Craft and Structure:

CCSS.ELA-LITERACY.RH.6-8.4

Determine the meaning of words and phrases as they are used in a text, including vocabulary specific to domains related to history/social studies.

CCSS.ELA-LITERACY.RH.6-8.5

Describe how a text presents information (e.g., sequentially, comparatively, causally).

CCSS.ELA-LITERACY.RH.6-8.6

Identify aspects of a text that reveal an author's point of view or purpose (e.g., loaded language, inclusion or avoidance of particular facts).

HISTORY & SOCIAL STUDIES

Integration of Knowledge and Ideas:

CCSS.ELA-LITERACY.RH.6-8.7

Integrate visual information (e.g., in charts, graphs, photographs, videos, or maps) with other information in print and digital texts.

CCSS.ELA-LITERACY.RH.6-8.8

Distinguish among fact, opinion, and reasoned judgment in a text.

CCSS.ELA-LITERACY.RH.6-8.9

Analyze the relationship between a primary and secondary source on the same topic.

Range of Reading and Level of Text Complexity:

CCSS.ELA-LITERACY.RH.6-8.10

By the end of grade 8, read and comprehend history/social studies texts in the grades 6-8 text complexity band independently and proficiently.

NAME:

SCORE:

SOURCE 1:

IS THIS A PRIMARY OR SECONDARY SOURCE?

EVIDENCE: _____

_____

EVIDENCE: _____

_____

SOURCE 1:

IS THIS A PRIMARY OR SECONDARY SOURCE?

EVIDENCE: _____

_____

EVIDENCE: _____

_____

RH.6-8.1: Cite specific textual evidence to support analysis of primary and secondary sources.

GRADE 7 WORKSHEETS: RH.6-8.2

NAME:

SCORE:

SOURCE:

IS THIS A PRIMARY OR SECONDARY SOURCE?

MAIN IDEA(S): _____

_____

SUMMARY: _____

_____

_____

_____

_____

_____

_____

_____

_____

_____

_____

RH.6-8.2: Determine the central ideas or information of a primary or secondary source; provide an accurate summary of the source distinct from prior knowledge or opinions.

NAME:

SCORE:

PROCESS:

STEPS/EVENTS:

#1 _____

#2 _____

#3 _____

#4 _____

#5 _____

#6 _____

COMMENTS: _____

_____

_____

_____

RH.6-8.3: Identify key steps in a text's description of a process related to history/social studies (e.g., how a bill becomes law, how interest rates are raised or lowered).

GRADE 7 WORKSHEETS: RH.6-8.4

NAME:

SCORE:

WORD/PHRASE:

SOURCE:

DEFINITION:

WORD/PHRASE:

SOURCE:

DEFINITION:

WORD/PHRASE:

SOURCE:

DEFINITION:

RH.6-8.4: Determine the meaning of words and phrases as they are used in a text, including vocabulary specific to domains related to history/social studies.

NAME:

SCORE:

SOURCE 1:

IN WHAT STYLE(S) IS THE MATERIAL PRESENTED?

EVIDENCE: _____

_____

EVIDENCE: _____

_____

SOURCE 2:

IN WHAT STYLE(S) IS THE MATERIAL PRESENTED?

EVIDENCE: _____

_____

EVIDENCE: _____

_____

RH.6-8.5: Describe how a text presents information (e.g., sequentially, comparatively, causally).

GRADE 7 WORKSHEETS: RH.6-8.6

NAME:

SCORE:

SOURCE 1:

POINT OF VIEW/PURPOSE:

EVIDENCE: _____

_____

EVIDENCE: _____

_____

SOURCE 2:

POINT OF VIEW/PURPOSE:

EVIDENCE: _____

_____

EVIDENCE: _____

_____

RH.6-8.6: Identify aspects of a text that reveal an author's point of view or purpose (e.g., loaded language, inclusion or avoidance of particular facts).

NAME:

SCORE:

SOURCE 1:

VISUAL ELEMENT:

HOW DOES THE VISUAL ELEMENT SUPPORT UNDERSTANDING OF THE TOPIC?

_____

_____

_____

SOURCE 2:

VISUAL ELEMENT:

HOW DOES THE VISUAL ELEMENT SUPPORT UNDERSTANDING OF THE TOPIC?

_____

_____

_____

RH.6-8.7: _Integrate visual information (e.g., in charts, graphs, photographs, videos, or maps) with other information in print and digital text_

NAME:

SCORE:

TOPIC:

VISUAL ELEMENT 1:

HOW WILL YOU USE THE ELEMENT IN YOUR REPORT?

_____

_____

VISUAL ELEMENT 2:

HOW WILL YOU USE THE ELEMENT IN YOUR REPORT?

_____

_____

VISUAL ELEMENT 3 (if needed):

HOW WILL YOU USE THE ELEMENT IN YOUR REPORT?

_____

_____

*COMPLETE YOUR REPORT/WRITING WITH THE ADDITION OF VISUAL ELEMENTS

RH.6-8.7: _SEE PAGE 1 FOR STANDARDS_

GRADE 7 WORKSHEETS: RH.6-8.8

NAME:

SCORE:

FACTUAL SOURCE:

FACT:

EVIDENCE:

OPINION SOURCE:

OPINION:

EVIDENCE:

REASONED JUDGEMENT SOURCE:

REASONED JUDGEMENT:

EVIDENCE:

RH.6-8.8: Distinguish among fact, opinion, and reasoned judgment in a text.

NAME: SCORE:

PRIMARY SOURCE:

SECONDARY SOURCE:

SIMILARITIES:

DIFFERENCES:

WHICH SOURCE IS MORE EFFECTIVE? WHY?

RH.6-8.9: Analyze the relationship between a primary and secondary source on the same topic.

NAME:

SCORE:

HISTORY/SOCIAL STUDIES TEXT:　　　　　　TOPIC(S):

#1 _____　　_____

HISTORY/SOCIAL STUDIES TEXT:　　　　　　TOPIC(S):

#2 _____　　_____

HISTORY/SOCIAL STUDIES TEXT:　　　　　　TOPIC(S):

#3 _____　　_____

HISTORY/SOCIAL STUDIES TEXT:　　　　　　TOPIC(S):

#4 _____　　_____

HISTORY/SOCIAL STUDIES TEXT:　　　　　　TOPIC(S):

#5 _____　　_____

HISTORY/SOCIAL STUDIES TEXT:　　　　　　TOPIC(S):

#6 _____　　_____

HISTORY/SOCIAL STUDIES TEXT:　　　　　　TOPIC(S):

#7 _____　　_____

RH.6-8.10: *By the end of grade 8, read and comprehend history/social studies texts in the grades 6-8 text complexity band independently and proficiently.*

SCIENCE & TECHNICAL SUBJECTS

SCIENCE & TECHNICAL SUBJECTS

Key Ideas and Details:

CCSS.ELA-LITERACY.RST.6-8.1

Cite specific textual evidence to support analysis of science and technical texts.

CCSS.ELA-LITERACY.RST.6-8.2

Determine the central ideas or conclusions of a text; provide an accurate summary of the text distinct from prior knowledge or opinions.

CCSS.ELA-LITERACY.RST.6-8.3

Follow precisely a multistep procedure when carrying out experiments, taking measurements, or performing technical tasks.

Craft and Structure:

CCSS.ELA-LITERACY.RST.6-8.4

Determine the meaning of symbols, key terms, and other domain-specific words and phrases as they are used in a specific scientific or technical context relevant to *grades 6-8 texts and topics*.

CCSS.ELA-LITERACY.RST.6-8.5

Analyze the structure an author uses to organize a text, including how the major sections contribute to the whole and to an understanding of the topic.

CCSS.ELA-LITERACY.RST.6-8.6

Analyze the author's purpose in providing an explanation, describing a procedure, or discussing an experiment in a text.

SCIENCE & TECHNICAL SUBJECTS

Integration of Knowledge and Ideas:

CCSS.ELA-LITERACY.RST.6-8.7

Integrate quantitative or technical information expressed in words in a text with a version of that information expressed visually (e.g., in a flowchart, diagram, model, graph, or table).

CCSS.ELA-LITERACY.RST.6-8.8

Distinguish among facts, reasoned judgment based on research findings, and speculation in a text.

CCSS.ELA-LITERACY.RST.6-8.9

Compare and contrast the information gained from experiments, simulations, video, or multimedia sources with that gained from reading a text on the same topic.

Range of Reading and Level of Text Complexity:

CCSS.ELA-LITERACY.RST.6-8.10

By the end of grade 8, read and comprehend science/technical texts in the grades 6-8 text complexity band independently and proficiently.

SOURCE:

KEY CONCEPT(S): _____

_____

_____

TEXT EVIDENCE: _____

_____

TEXT EVIDENCE: _____

_____

TEXT EVIDENCE: _____

_____

TEXT EVIDENCE: _____

_____

RST.6-8.1: Cite specific textual evidence to support analysis of science and technical texts.

NAME:

SCORE:

SOURCE:

KEY CONCEPT(S): _____

_____

_____

SUMMARY: _____

_____

_____

_____

_____

_____

_____

_____

_____

_____

RST.6-8.2: Determine the central ideas or conclusions of a text; provide an accurate summary of the text distinct from prior knowledge or opinions.

GRADE 7 WORKSHEETS: RST.6-8.3

PROCEDURE:

STEPS:

#1 _____

#2 _____

#3 _____

#4 _____

#5 _____

#6 _____

MEASUREMENTS/DATA/COMMENTS: _____

_____

_____

RST.6-8.3: *Follow precisely a multistep procedure when carrying out experiments, taking measurements, or performing technical tasks.*

SYMBOL/KEY TERM:

SOURCE:

DEFINITION:

SYMBOL/KEY TERM:

SOURCE:

DEFINITION:

SYMBOL/KEY TERM:

SOURCE:

DEFINITION:

RST.6-8.4: Determine the meaning of symbols, key terms, and other domain-specific words and phrases as they are used in a specific scientific or technical context relevant to grades 6-8 texts and topics.

GRADE 7 WORKSHEETS: RST.6-8.5

NAME:

SCORE:

SOURCE 1:

HOW IS THE TEXT ORGANIZED?

HOW DOES THIS HELP THE READER TO UNDERSTAND THE TOPIC?

SOURCE 2:

HOW IS THE TEXT ORGANIZED?

HOW DOES THIS HELP THE READER TO UNDERSTAND THE TOPIC?

RST.6-8.5: *Analyze the structure an author uses to organize a text, including how the major sections contribute to the whole and to an understanding of the topic.*

GRADE 7 WORKSHEETS: RST.6-8.6

NAME:

SCORE:

PROCEDURE/EXPERIMENT:

AUTHOR'S PURPOSE:

EVIDENCE:

EVIDENCE:

EXPLANATION:

AUTHOR'S PURPOSE:

EVIDENCE:

EVIDENCE:

RST.6-8.6: *Analyze the author's purpose in providing an explanation, describing a procedure, or discussing an experiment in a text.*

GRADE 7 WORKSHEETS: RST.6-8.7 (page 1)

NAME:

SCORE:

SOURCE 1:

VISUAL ELEMENT:

HOW DOES THE VISUAL ELEMENT SUPPORT UNDERSTANDING OF THE TOPIC?

_____

_____

_____

SOURCE 2:

VISUAL ELEMENT:

HOW DOES THE VISUAL ELEMENT SUPPORT UNDERSTANDING OF THE TOPIC?

_____

_____

_____

RST.6-8.7: *Integrate quantitative or technical information expressed in words in a text with a version of that information expressed visually (e.g., in a flowchart, diagram, model, graph, or table).*

NAME:

SCORE:

TOPIC:

VISUAL ELEMENT 1:

HOW WILL YOU USE THE ELEMENT IN YOUR REPORT?

_____

_____

VISUAL ELEMENT 2:

HOW WILL YOU USE THE ELEMENT IN YOUR REPORT?

_____

_____

VISUAL ELEMENT 3 (if needed):

HOW WILL YOU USE THE ELEMENT IN YOUR REPORT?

_____

_____

*COMPLETE YOUR REPORT/WRITING WITH THE ADDITION OF VISUAL ELEMENTS

RST.6-8.7: SEE PAGE 1 FOR STANDARDS

GRADE 7 WORKSHEETS: RST.6-8.8

NAME:

SCORE:

FACTUAL SOURCE:

FACT:

EVIDENCE:

SPECULATIVE SOURCE:

SPECULATION:

EVIDENCE:

REASONED JUDGEMENT SOURCE:

REASONED JUDGEMENT:

EVIDENCE:

RST.6-8.8: Distinguish among facts, reasoned judgment based on research findings, and speculation in a text.

NAME:

SCORE:

MULTIMEDIA SOURCE:

TEXT SOURCE:

SIMILARITIES:

DIFFERENCES:

WHICH SOURCE IS MORE EFFECTIVE? WHY?

RST.6-8.9: *Compare and contrast the information gained from experiments, simulations, video, or multimedia sources with that gained from reading a text on the same topic.*

NAME:

SCORE:

SCIENCE/TECHNICAL TEXT: **TOPIC(S):**

#1 _____   _____

SCIENCE/TECHNICAL TEXT: **TOPIC(S):**

#2 _____   _____

SCIENCE/TECHNICAL TEXT: **TOPIC(S):**

#3 _____   _____

SCIENCE/TECHNICAL TEXT: **TOPIC(S):**

#4 _____   _____

SCIENCE/TECHNICAL TEXT: **TOPIC(S):**

#5 _____   _____

SCIENCE/TECHNICAL TEXT: **TOPIC(S):**

#6 _____   _____

SCIENCE/TECHNICAL TEXT: **TOPIC(S):**

#7 _____   _____

RH.6-8.10: By the end of grade 8, read and comprehend science/technical texts in the grades 6-8 text complexity band independently and proficiently.

RATIOS & PROPORTIONAL RELATIONSHIPS

RATIOS & PROPORTIONAL RELATIONSHIPS

Analyze proportional relationships and use them to solve real-world and mathematical problems:

CCSS.MATH.CONTENT.7.RP.A.1

Compute unit rates associated with ratios of fractions, including ratios of lengths, areas and other quantities measured in like or different units. *For example, if a person walks 1/2 mile in each 1/4 hour, compute the unit rate as the complex fraction 1/2/1/4 miles per hour, equivalently 2 miles per hour.*

CCSS.MATH.CONTENT.7.RP.A.2

Recognize and represent proportional relationships between quantities.

- CCSS.MATH.CONTENT.7.RP.A.2.A

Decide whether two quantities are in a proportional relationship, e.g., by testing for equivalent ratios in a table or graphing on a coordinate plane and observing whether the graph is a straight line through the origin.

- CCSS.MATH.CONTENT.7.RP.A.2.B

Identify the constant of proportionality (unit rate) in tables, graphs, equations, diagrams, and verbal descriptions of proportional relationships.

- CCSS.MATH.CONTENT.7.RP.A.2.C

Represent proportional relationships by equations. *For example, if total cost t is proportional to the number n of items purchased at a constant price p, the relationship between the total cost and the number of items can be expressed as t = pn.*

- CCSS.MATH.CONTENT.7.RP.A.2.D

Explain what a point (x, y) on the graph of a proportional relationship means in terms of the situation, with special attention to the points $(0, 0)$ and $(1, r)$ where r is the unit rate.

RATIOS & PROPORTIONAL RELATIONSHIPS

Analyze proportional relationships and use them to solve real-world and mathematical problems (continued):

CCSS.MATH.CONTENT.7.RP.A.3

Use proportional relationships to solve multistep ratio and percent problems. Examples: simple interest, tax, markups and markdowns, gratuities and commissions, fees, percent increase and decrease, percent error.

NAME:

SCORE:

QUANTITY 1:

QUANTITY 2:

RATIO:

HOW ARE THE TWO QUANTITIES RELATED? _____

_____

QUANTITY 1:

QUANTITY 2:

RATIO:

HOW ARE THE TWO QUANTITIES RELATED? _____

_____

7.RP.A.1: Compute unit rates associated with ratios of fractions, including ratios of lengths, areas and other quantities measured in like or different units. For example, if a person walks 1/2 mile in each 1/4 hour, compute the unit rate as the complex fraction 1/2/1/4 miles per hour, equivalently 2 miles per hour.

GRADE 7 WORKSHEETS:7.RP.A.2.A

NAME:

SCORE:

PROBLEM & WORK SPACE:

SOLUTIONS:

UNIT RATES:

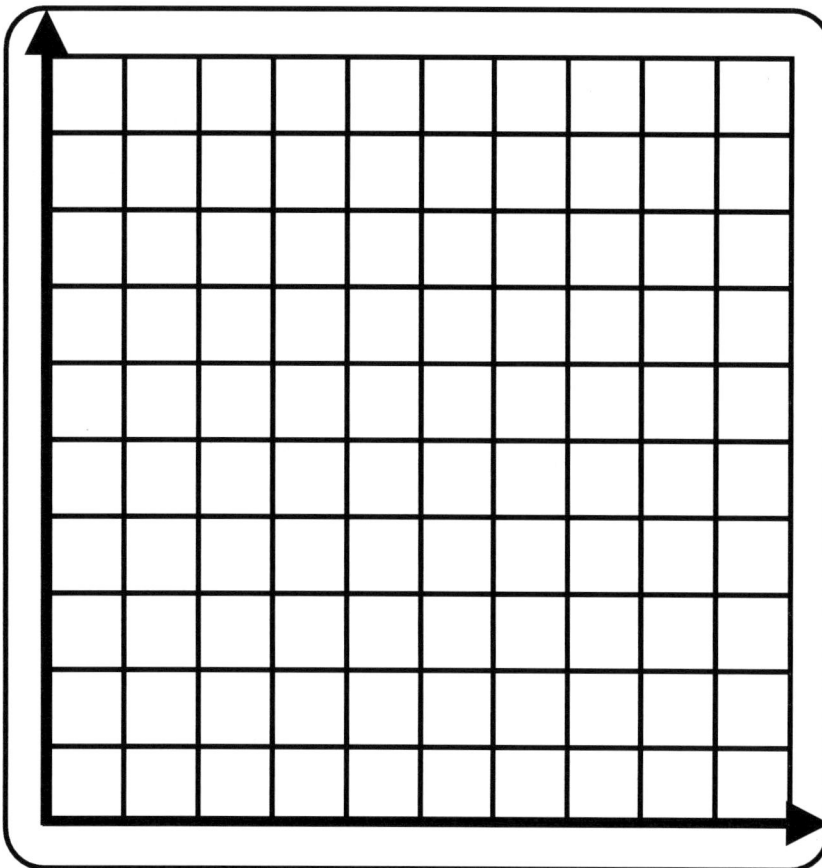

ABC	X	Y

7.RP.A.2.A: *Recognize and represent proportional relationships between quantities. Decide whether two quantities are in a proportional relationship, e.g., by testing for equivalent ratios in a table or graphing on a coordinate plane and observing whether the graph is a straight line through the origin.*

GRADE 7 WORKSHEETS:7.RP.A.2.B

NAME:

SCORE:

PROBLEM & WORK SPACE:

SOLUTIONS:

UNIT RATES:

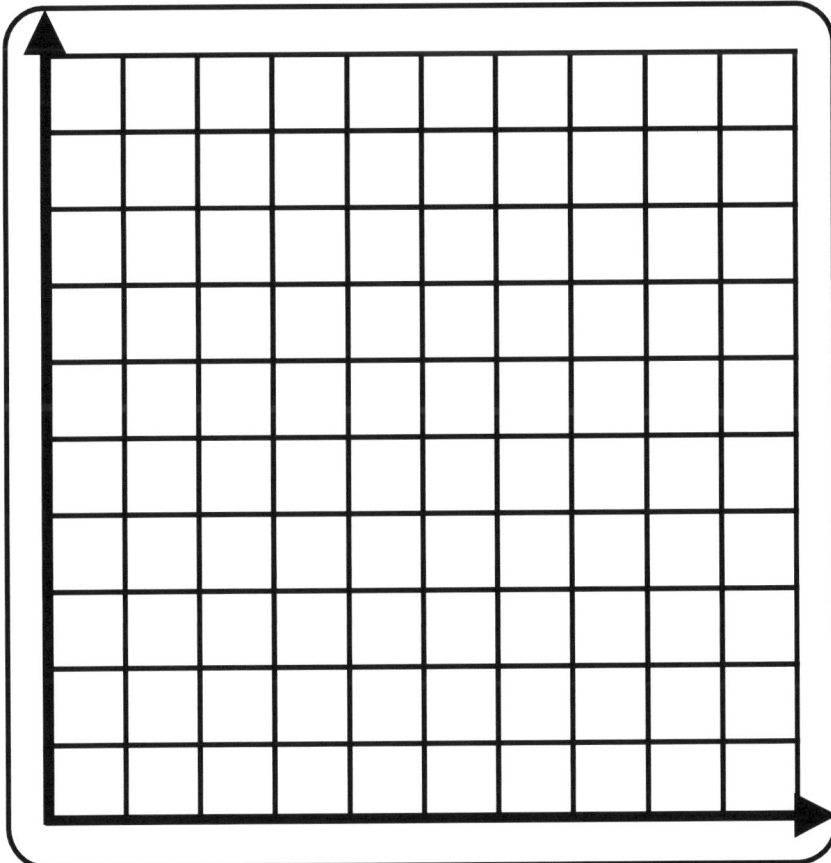

ABC	X	Y

7.RP.A.2.B: *Identify the constant of proportionality (unit rate) in tables, graphs, equations, diagrams, and verbal descriptions of proportional relationships.*

NAME:

SCORE:

PROBLEM & WORK SPACE:

EQUATION:

PROBLEM & WORK SPACE:

EQUATION:

PROBLEM & WORK SPACE:

EQUATION:

7.RP.A.2.C: Represent proportional relationships by equations. For example, if total cost t is proportional to the number n of items purchased at a constant price p, the relationship between the total cost and the number of items can be expressed as t = pn.

NAME:

SCORE:

STORY/PROBLEM:

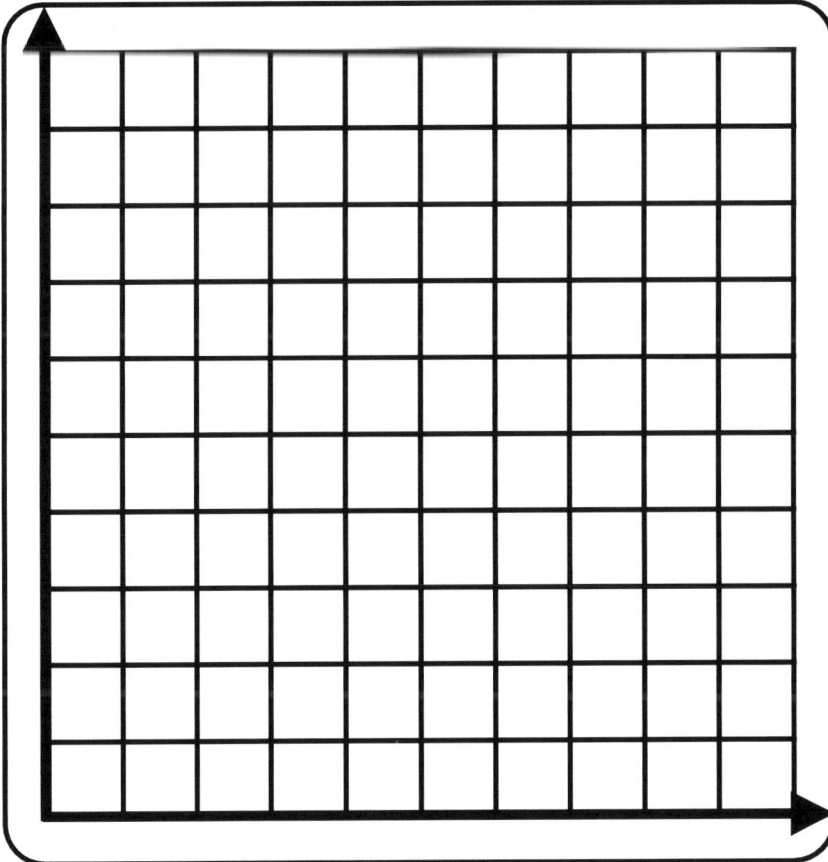

ABC	X	Y

EXPLAIN THE MEANING OF POINT _____:

EXPLAIN THE MEANING OF POINT _____:

7.RP.A.2.D: *Explain what a point (x, y) on the graph of a proportional relationship means in terms of the situation, with special attention to the points (0, 0) and (1, r) where r is the unit rate.*

NAME:

SCORE:

PROBLEM:

RATES/RATIOS:

WORK SPACE:

SOLUTION:

PROBLEM:

RATES/RATIOS:

WORK SPACE:

SOLUTION:

6.RP.A.3: *Use proportional relationships to solve multistep ratio and percent problems. Examples: simple interest, tax, markups and markdowns, gratuities and commissions, fees, percent increase and decrease, percent error.*

THE
NUMBER
SYSTEM

THE NUMBER SYSTEM

Apply and extend previous understandings of operations with fractions:

CCSS.MATH.CONTENT.7.NS.A.1

Apply and extend previous understandings of addition and subtraction to add and subtract rational numbers; represent addition and subtraction on a horizontal or vertical number line diagram.

• CCSS.MATH.CONTENT.7.NS.A.1.A

Describe situations in which opposite quantities combine to make 0. *For example, a hydrogen atom has 0 charge because its two constituents are oppositely charged.*

• CCSS.MATH.CONTENT.7.NS.A.1.B

Understand $p + q$ as the number located a distance $|q|$ from p, in the positive or negative direction depending on whether q is positive or negative. Show that a number and its opposite have a sum of 0 (are additive inverses). Interpret sums of rational numbers by describing real-world contexts.

• CCSS.MATH.CONTENT.7.NS.A.1.C

Understand subtraction of rational numbers as adding the additive inverse, $p - q = p + (-q)$. Show that the distance between two rational numbers on the number line is the absolute value of their difference, and apply this principle in real-world contexts.

• CCSS.MATH.CONTENT.7.NS.A.1.D

Apply properties of operations as strategies to add and subtract rational numbers.

THE NUMBER SYSTEM

Apply and extend previous understandings of operations with fractions (continued):

CCSS.MATH.CONTENT.7.NS.A.2

Apply and extend previous understandings of multiplication and division and of fractions to multiply and divide rational numbers.

• CCSS.MATH.CONTENT.7.NS.A.2.A

Understand that multiplication is extended from fractions to rational numbers by requiring that operations continue to satisfy the properties of operations, particularly the distributive property, leading to products such as (-1)(-1) = 1 and the rules for multiplying signed numbers. Interpret products of rational numbers by describing real-world contexts.

• CCSS.MATH.CONTENT.7.NS.A.2.B

Understand that integers can be divided, provided that the divisor is not zero, and every quotient of integers (with non-zero divisor) is a rational number. If p and q are integers, then $-(p/q) = (-p)/q = p/(-q)$. Interpret quotients of rational numbers by describing real-world contexts.

• CCSS.MATH.CONTENT.7.NS.A.2.C

Apply properties of operations as strategies to multiply and divide rational numbers.

• CCSS.MATH.CONTENT.7.NS.A.2.D

Convert a rational number to a decimal using long division; know that the decimal form of a rational number terminates in 0s or eventually repeats.

CCSS.MATH.CONTENT.7.NS.A.3

Solve real-world and mathematical problems involving the four operations with rational numbers.

GRADE 7 WORKSHEETS:7.NS.A.1.A

NAME:

SCORE:

STORY/PROBLEM: _____

_____

NUMBER 1:	+	NUMBER 2:	=	SOLUTION:

USE THE NUMBER LINE TO EXPRESS THE PROBLEM:

STORY/PROBLEM:

_____

NUMBER 1:	+	NUMBER 2:	=	SOLUTION:

USE THE NUMBER LINE TO EXPRESS THE PROBLEM:

7.NS.A.1.A: *Apply and extend previous understandings of addition and subtraction to add and subtract rational numbers; represent addition and subtraction on a horizontal or vertical number line diagram. Describe situations in which opposite quantities combine to make 0. For example, a hydrogen atom has 0 charge because its two constituents are oppositely charged.*

GRADE 7 WORKSHEETS:7.NS.A.1.B

NAME:

SCORE:

NUMBER:

+

OPPOSITE:

=

0

FIND THE NUMBER AND ITS OPPOSITE ON THE NUMBER LINE:

REAL WORLD EXAMPLE:

NUMBER:

+

OPPOSITE:

=

0

FIND THE NUMBER AND ITS OPPOSITE ON THE NUMBER LINE:

REAL WORLD EXAMPLE:

7.NS.A.1.B: *Understand p + q as the number located a distance |q| from p, in the positive or negative direction depending on whether q is positive or negative. Show that a number and its opposite have a sum of 0 (are additive inverses). Interpret sums of rational numbers by describing real-world contexts.*

GRADE 7 WORKSHEETS: 7.NS.A.1.C

NAME:

SCORE:

NUMBER:

OPPOSITE:

DISTANCE BETWEEN THEM:

FIND THE NUMBER AND ITS OPPOSITE ON THE NUMBER LINE:

⟵————————————————————⟶

REAL WORLD EXAMPLE:

NUMBER:

OPPOSITE:

DISTANCE BETWEEN THEM:

FIND THE NUMBER AND ITS OPPOSITE ON THE NUMBER LINE:

⟵————————————————————⟶

REAL WORLD EXAMPLE:

7.NS.A.1.C: *Understand subtraction of rational numbers as adding the additive inverse, p - q = p+ (-q). Show that the distance between two rational numbers on the number line is the absolute value of their difference, and apply this principle in real-world contexts.*

NAME:

SCORE:

	+		=		
	+		=		
	+		=		
	+		=		
	+		=		
	-		=		
	-		=		
	-		=		
	-		=		

7.NS.A.1.D: *Apply properties of operations as strategies to add and subtract rational numbers.*

NAME:

SCORE:

[ ] X [ ] = [ ]

REAL WORLD EXAMPLE:

[ ] ÷ [ ] = [ ]

REAL WORLD EXAMPLE:

[ ] [ ] = [ ]

REAL WORLD EXAMPLE:

7.NS.A.2.A: Apply and extend previous understandings of multiplication and division and of fractions to multiply and divide rational numbers. Understand that multiplication is extended from fractions to rational numbers by requiring that operations continue to satisfy the properties of operations, particularly the distributive property, leading to products such as (-1)(-1) = 1 and the rules for multiplying signed numbers. Interpret products of rational numbers by describing real-world contexts.

GRADE 7 WORKSHEETS: 7.NS.A.2.B-C

NAME:

SCORE:

[ ] X [ ] = [ ]

STRATEGIES USED:

REAL WORLD EXAMPLE:

[ ] ÷ [ ] = [ ]

STRATEGIES USED:

REAL WORLD EXAMPLE:

[ ] [ ] = [ ]

STRATEGIES USED:

REAL WORLD EXAMPLE:

7.NS.A.2.B: *Understand that integers can be divided, provided that the divisor is not zero, and every quotient of integers (with non-zero divisor) is a rational number. If p and q are integers, then -(p/q) = (-p)/q = p/(-q). Interpret quotients of rational numbers by describing real-world contexts.*

7.NS.A.2.C: *Apply properties of operations as strategies to multiply and divide rational numbers.*

REPEATING OR TERMINATING DECIMAL?

REPEATING OR TERMINATING DECIMAL?

REPEATING OR TERMINATING DECIMAL?

REPEATING OR TERMINATING DECIMAL?

7.NS.A.2.D: *Convert a rational number to a decimal using long division; know that the decimal form of a rational number terminates in 0s or eventually repeats.*

GRADE 7 WORKSHEETS:7.NS.A.3

NAME:

SCORE:

#1

SOLUTION:

#2

SOLUTION:

#3

SOLUTION:

#4

SOLUTION:

#5

SOLUTION:

#6

SOLUTION:

7.NS.A.3: *Solve real-world and mathematical problems involving the four operations with rational numbers.*

EXPRESSIONS & EQUATIONS

EXPRESSIONS & EQUATIONS

Use properties of operations to generate equivalent expressions:

CCSS.MATH.CONTENT.7.EE.A.1

Apply properties of operations as strategies to add, subtract, factor, and expand linear expressions with rational coefficients.

CCSS.MATH.CONTENT.7.EE.A.2

Understand that rewriting an expression in different forms in a problem context can shed light on the problem and how the quantities in it are related. *For example, a + 0.05a = 1.05a means that "increase by 5%" is the same as "multiply by 1.05."*

Solve real-life and mathematical problems using numerical and algebraic expressions and equations:

CCSS.MATH.CONTENT.7.EE.B.3

Solve multi-step real-life and mathematical problems posed with positive and negative rational numbers in any form (whole numbers, fractions, and decimals), using tools strategically. Apply properties of operations to calculate with numbers in any form; convert between forms as appropriate; and assess the reasonableness of answers using mental computation and estimation strategies. *For example: If a woman making $25 an hour gets a 10% raise, she will make an additional 1/10 of her salary an hour, or $2.50, for a new salary of $27.50. If you want to place a towel bar 9 3/4 inches long in the center of a door that is 27 1/2 inches wide, you will need to place the bar about 9 inches from each edge; this estimate can be used as a check on the exact computation.*

EXPRESSIONS & EQUATIONS

Solve real-life and mathematical problems using numerical and algebraic expressions and equations (continued):

CCSS.MATH.CONTENT.7.EE.B.4

Use variables to represent quantities in a real-world or mathematical problem, and construct simple equations and inequalities to solve problems by reasoning about the quantities.

- CCSS.MATH.CONTENT.7.EE.B.4.A

Solve word problems leading to equations of the form $px + q = r$ and $p(x + q) = r$, where p, q, and r are specific rational numbers. Solve equations of these forms fluently. Compare an algebraic solution to an arithmetic solution, identifying the sequence of the operations used in each approach. *For example, the perimeter of a rectangle is 54 cm. Its length is 6 cm. What is its width?*

- CCSS.MATH.CONTENT.7.EE.B.4.B

Solve word problems leading to inequalities of the form $px + q > r$ or $px + q < r$, where p, q, and r are specific rational numbers. Graph the solution set of the inequality and interpret it in the context of the problem. *For example: As a salesperson, you are paid $50 per week plus $3 per sale. This week you want your pay to be at least $100. Write an inequality for the number of sales you need to make, and describe the solutions.*

NAME:

SCORE:

EQUATION:

STEP 1:

STEP 2:

STEP 3:

STEP 4:

STEP 5:

SOLUTION:

7.EE.A.1: *Apply properties of operations as strategies to add, subtract, factor, and expand linear expressions with rational coefficients.*

NAME:

SCORE:

EQUATION:

REWRITE EQUATION:

EXPLAIN THE DIFFERENCE: _____

_____

EQUATION:

REWRITE EQUATION:

EXPLAIN THE DIFFERENCE: _____

_____

7.EE.A.2: *Understand that rewriting an expression in different forms in a problem context can shed light on the problem and how the quantities in it are related. For example, a + 0.05a = 1.05a means that "increase by 5%" is the same as "multiply by 1.05."*

GRADE 7 WORKSHEETS: 7.EE.B.3

NAME:

SCORE:

STORY/PROBLEM:

STEP 1:

STEP 2:

STEP 3:

STEP 4:

ILLUSTRATE AS NEEDED:

SOLUTION:

7.EE.B.3: *Solve multi-step real-life and mathematical problems posed with positive and negative rational numbers in any form (whole numbers, fractions, and decimals), using tools strategically. Apply properties of operations to calculate with numbers in any form; convert between forms as appropriate; and assess the reasonableness of answers using mental computation and estimation strategies. For example: If a woman making $25 an hour gets a 10% raise, she will make an additional 1/10 of her salary an hour, or $2.50, for a new salary of $27.50. If you want to place a towel bar 9 3/4 inches long in the center of a door that is 27 1/2 inches wide, you will need to place the bar about 9 inches from each edge; this estimate can be used as a check on the exact computation.*

NAME:

SCORE:

EQUATION:

GIVEN VALUES:

SOLUTION/WORK SPACE:

FORMULA:

GIVEN VALUES:

SOLUTION/WORK SPACE:

7.EE.B.4.A: Use variables to represent quantities in a real-world or mathematical problem, and construct simple equations and inequalities to solve problems by reasoning about the quantities.Solve word problems leading to equations of the form px + q = r and p(x + q) = r, where p, q, and r are specific rational numbers. Solve equations of these forms fluently. Compare an algebraic solution to an arithmetic solution, identifying the sequence of the operations used in each approach. For example, the perimeter of a rectangle is 54 cm. Its length is 6 cm. What is its width?

NAME:

SCORE:

GRAPHING SPACE:

DATA TABLE:

PROBLEM:

EQUATION:

VARIABLES:

7.EE.B.4.B: *Solve word problems leading to inequalities of the form px + q > r or px + q < r, where p, q, and r are specific rational numbers. Graph the solution set of the inequality and interpret it in the context of the problem. For example: As a salesperson, you are paid $50 per week plus $3 per sale. This week you want your pay to be at least $100. Write an inequality for the number of sales you need to make, and describe the solutions.*

GEOMETRY

GEOMETRY

Draw construct, and describe geometrical figures and describe the relationships between them:

CCSS.MATH.CONTENT.7.G.A.1

Solve problems involving scale drawings of geometric figures, including computing actual lengths and areas from a scale drawing and reproducing a scale drawing at a different scale.

CCSS.MATH.CONTENT.7.G.A.2

Draw (freehand, with ruler and protractor, and with technology) geometric shapes with given conditions. Focus on constructing triangles from three measures of angles or sides, noticing when the conditions determine a unique triangle, more than one triangle, or no triangle.

CCSS.MATH.CONTENT.7.G.A.3

Describe the two-dimensional figures that result from slicing three-dimensional figures, as in plane sections of right rectangular prisms and right rectangular pyramids.

GEOMETRY

Solve real-life and mathematical problems involving angle measure, area, surface area, and volume:

CCSS.MATH.CONTENT.7.G.B.4

Know the formulas for the area and circumference of a circle and use them to solve problems; give an informal derivation of the relationship between the circumference and area of a circle.

CCSS.MATH.CONTENT.7.G.B.5

Use facts about supplementary, complementary, vertical, and adjacent angles in a multi-step problem to write and solve simple equations for an unknown angle in a figure.

CCSS.MATH.CONTENT.7.G.B.6

Solve real-world and mathematical problems involving area, volume and surface area of two- and three-dimensional objects composed of triangles, quadrilaterals, polygons, cubes, and right prisms.

NAME:

SCORE:

PROBLEM:

ORIGINAL SHAPE:

SHAPE AT INCREASED SCALE:

FORMULA(S):

SOLUTIONS/LENGTHS/MEASURES:

7.G.A.1: *Solve problems involving scale drawings of geometric figures, including computing actual lengths and areas from a scale drawing and reproducing a scale drawing at a different scale.*

GRADE 7 WORKSHEETS: 7.G.A.2

NAME:

SCORE:

REQUIREMENTS:

DRAW THE SHAPE:

REQUIREMENTS:

DRAW THE SHAPE:

7.G.A.2: Draw (freehand, with ruler and protractor, and with technology) geometric shapes with given conditions. Focus on constructing triangles from three measures of angles or sides, noticing when the conditions determine a unique triangle, more than one triangle, or no triangle.

GRADE 7 WORKSHEETS: 7.G.A.3

NAME:

SCORE:

3D FIGURE:

PIECE OF 3D FIGURE:

DESCRIBE THE RESULTING SHAPE/FIGURE: _____

_____

3D FIGURE:

PIECE OF 3D FIGURE:

DESCRIBE THE RESULTING SHAPE/FIGURE: _____

_____

7.G.A.3: Describe the two-dimensional figures that result from slicing three-dimensional figures, as in plane sections of right rectangular prisms and right rectangular pyramids.

NAME:

SCORE:

CIRCUMFERENCE FORMULA:

AREA FORMULA:

PI=

CIRCLE:

AREA:

CIRCUMFERENCE:

CIRCLE:

AREA:

CIRCUMFERENCE:

7.G.B.4: *Know the formulas for the area and circumference of a circle and use them to solve problems; give an informal derivation of the relationship between the circumference and area of a circle.*

MIDDLE SCHOOL COMMON CORE ASSESSMENTS (C) 2015 Andrew Frinkle

GRADE 7 WORKSHEETS:7.G.B.5

NAME:

SCORE:

COMPLEMENTARY ANGLES =

SUPPLEMENTARY ANGLES =

ANGLES:

FIND MEASURES FOR ALL
UNKNOWN ANGLES:

ANGLES:

FIND MEASURES FOR ALL
UNKNOWN ANGLES:

7.G.B.5: Use facts about supplementary, complementary, vertical, and adjacent angles in a multi-step problem to write and solve simple equations for an unknown angle in a figure.

NAME:

SCORE:

2D SHAPE(S):

FORMULAS:

FIND THE AREA(S):

2D SHAPE(S):

FORMULAS:

FIND THE AREA(S):

7.G.B.6: *Solve real-world and mathematical problems involving area, volume and surface area of two- and three-dimensional objects composed of triangles, quadrilaterals, polygons, cubes, and right prisms.*

NAME:

SCORE:

3D FIGURE(S):

FORMULAS:

FIND THE VOLUME(S):

3D FIGURE(S):

FORMULAS:

FIND THE SURFACE AREA(S):

7.G.B.6: *SEE PAGE 1 FOR STANDARDS AND EXPECTATIONS*

STATISTICS & PROBABILITY

STATISTICS & PROBABILITY

Use random sampling to draw inferences about a population:

CCSS.MATH.CONTENT.7.SP.A.1

Understand that statistics can be used to gain information about a population by examining a sample of the population; generalizations about a population from a sample are valid only if the sample is representative of that population. Understand that random sampling tends to produce representative samples and support valid inferences.

CCSS.MATH.CONTENT.7.SP.A.2

Use data from a random sample to draw inferences about a population with an unknown characteristic of interest. Generate multiple samples (or simulated samples) of the same size to gauge the variation in estimates or predictions. *For example, estimate the mean word length in a book by randomly sampling words from the book; predict the winner of a school election based on randomly sampled survey data. Gauge how far off the estimate or prediction might be.*

STATISTICS & PROBABILITY

Draw informal comparative inferences about two populations:

CCSS.MATH.CONTENT.7.SP.B.3

Informally assess the degree of visual overlap of two numerical data distributions with similar variabilities, measuring the difference between the centers by expressing it as a multiple of a measure of variability. *For example, the mean height of players on the basketball team is 10 cm greater than the mean height of players on the soccer team, about twice the variability (mean absolute deviation) on either team; on a dot plot, the separation between the two distributions of heights is noticeable.*

CCSS.MATH.CONTENT.7.SP.B.4

Use measures of center and measures of variability for numerical data from random samples to draw informal comparative inferences about two populations. *For example, decide whether the words in a chapter of a seventh-grade science book are generally longer than the words in a chapter of a fourth-grade science book.*

GRADE 7 STANDARDS

STATISTICS & PROBABILITY

Investigate chance processes and develop, use, and evaluate probability models:

CCSS.MATH.CONTENT.7.SP.C.5

Understand that the probability of a chance event is a number between 0 and 1 that expresses the likelihood of the event occurring. Larger numbers indicate greater likelihood. A probability near 0 indicates an unlikely event, a probability around 1/2 indicates an event that is neither unlikely nor likely, and a probability near 1 indicates a likely event.

CCSS.MATH.CONTENT.7.SP.C.6

Approximate the probability of a chance event by collecting data on the chance process that produces it and observing its long-run relative frequency, and predict the approximate relative frequency given the probability. *For example, when rolling a number cube 600 times, predict that a 3 or 6 would be rolled roughly 200 times, but probably not exactly 200 times.*

STATISTICS & PROBABILITY

Investigate chance processes and develop, use, and evaluate probability models (continued):

CCSS.MATH.CONTENT.7.SP.C.7

Develop a probability model and use it to find probabilities of events. Compare probabilities from a model to observed frequencies; if the agreement is not good, explain possible sources of the discrepancy.

- CCSS.MATH.CONTENT.7.SP.C.7.A

Develop a uniform probability model by assigning equal probability to all outcomes, and use the model to determine probabilities of events. *For example, if a student is selected at random from a class, find the probability that Jane will be selected and the probability that a girl will be selected.*

- CCSS.MATH.CONTENT.7.SP.C.7.B

Develop a probability model (which may not be uniform) by observing frequencies in data generated from a chance process. *For example, find the approximate probability that a spinning penny will land heads up or that a tossed paper cup will land open-end down. Do the outcomes for the spinning penny appear to be equally likely based on the observed frequencies?*

STATISTICS & PROBABILITY

Investigate chance processes and develop, use, and evaluate probability models (continued):

CCSS.MATH.CONTENT.7.SP.C.8

Find probabilities of compound events using organized lists, tables, tree diagrams, and simulation.

- CCSS.MATH.CONTENT.7.SP.C.8.A

Understand that, just as with simple events, the probability of a compound event is the fraction of outcomes in the sample space for which the compound event occurs.

- CCSS.MATH.CONTENT.7.SP.C.8.B

Represent sample spaces for compound events using methods such as organized lists, tables and tree diagrams. For an event described in everyday language (e.g., "rolling double sixes"), identify the outcomes in the sample space which compose the event.

- CCSS.MATH.CONTENT.7.SP.C.8.C

Design and use a simulation to generate frequencies for compound events. *For example, use random digits as a simulation tool to approximate the answer to the question: If 40% of donors have type A blood, what is the probability that it will take at least 4 donors to find one with type A blood?*

GRADE 7 WORKSHEETS: 7.SP.A.1

NAME:

SCORE:

QUESTION:

CATEGORY	VALUE

GRAPH THE DATA:

WAS THE DATA REPRESENTATIVE OF THE POPULATION? WHY OR WHY NOT?

_____

_____

WHAT CONCLUSIONS/INFERENCES CAN YOU MAKE ABOUT THE DATA?

_____

_____

7.SP.A.1: Understand that statistics can be used to gain information about a population by examining a sample of the population; generalizations about a population from a sample are valid only if the sample is representative of that population. Understand that random sampling tends to produce representative samples and support valid inferences.

GRADE 7 WORKSHEETS: 7.SP.A.2

NAME:

SCORE:

QUESTION:

CATEGORY	VALUE

GRAPH THE DATA:

MAKE PREDICTIONS ABOUT THE ACCURACY OF THE DATA SAMPLE:

_____

_____

_____

7.SP.A.2: Use data from a random sample to draw inferences about a population with an unknown characteristic of interest. Generate multiple samples (or simulated samples) of the same size to gauge the variation in estimates or predictions. For example, estimate the mean word length in a book by randomly sampling words from the book; predict the winner of a school election based on randomly sampled survey data. Gauge how far off the estimate or prediction might be.

NAME:

SCORE:

DATA TO COMPARE:

DATA GRAPH #1

DATA GRAPH #2

COMPARE THE DISTRIBUTIONS OF DATA ON BOTH GRAPHS:

_____

_____

7.SP.B.3: *Informally assess the degree of visual overlap of two numerical data distributions with similar variabilities, measuring the difference between the centers by expressing it as a multiple of a measure of variability. For example, the mean height of players on the basketball team is 10 cm greater than the mean height of players on the soccer team, about twice the variability (mean absolute deviation) on either team; on a dot plot, the separation between the two distributions of heights is noticeable.*

GRADE 7 WORKSHEETS: 7.SP.B.3 (page 2)

NAME:

SCORE:

DATA TO COMPARE:

GRAPH 2 DATA SETS ON 1 GRAPH:

GRAPH KEY:

COMPARE THE DISTRIBUTIONS OF DATA ON THE GRAPH:

_____

_____

_____

_____

7.SP.B.3: *SEE PAGE 1 FOR STANDARDS AND EXPECTATIONS*

GRADE 7 WORKSHEETS: 7.SP.B.4

NAME:

SCORE:

DATA BEING GRAPHED:

CATEGORY	VALUE

GRAPH THE DATA:

MEASURES OF VARIABILITY:

USE MEAN, MEDIAN, MODE, DEVIATION, AND OTHER MEASURES TO COMPARE DATA:

_____

_____

_____

7.SP.B.4: Use measures of center and measures of variability for numerical data from random samples to draw informal comparative inferences about two populations. For example, decide whether the words in a chapter of a seventh-grade science book are generally longer than the words in a chapter of a fourth-grade science book.

NAME:

SCORE:

GRAPH ITEMS ACCORDING TO PROBABILITY OF OCCURRENCE:

UNLIKELY

LIKELY

0

1

ITEM:

PROBABILITY:

7.SP.C.5: *Understand that the probability of a chance event is a number between 0 and 1 that expresses the likelihood of the event occurring. Larger numbers indicate greater likelihood. A probability near 0 indicates an unlikely event, a probability around 1/2 indicates an event that is neither unlikely nor likely, and a probability near 1 indicates a likely event.*

GRADE 7 WORKSHEETS:7.SP.C.6

NAME:

SCORE:

DATA BEING GRAPHED:

OUTCOME	VALUE	RATE

GRAPH THE DATA:

PREDICTIONS:

_____

_____

OBSERVATIONS ABOUT RESULTS:

_____

_____

7.SP.C.6: Approximate the probability of a chance event by collecting data on the chance process that produces it and observing its long-run relative frequency, and predict the approximate relative frequency given the probability. For example, when rolling a number cube 600 times, predict that a 3 or 6 would be rolled roughly 200 times, but probably not exactly 200 times.

NAME:

SCORE:

DATA BEING GRAPHED:

OUTCOME	VALUE	PREDICTED	ACTUAL

REFLECTIONS ABOUT ACCURACIES/INACCURACIES:

_____

_____

_____

7.SP.C.7.A: Develop a probability model and use it to find probabilities of events. Compare probabilities from a model to observed frequencies; if the agreement is not good, explain possible sources of the discrepancy. Develop a uniform probability model by assigning equal probability to all outcomes, and use the model to determine probabilities of events. For example, if a student is selected at random from a class, find the probability that Jane will be selected and the probability that a girl will be selected.

7.SP.C.7.B: Develop a probability model (which may not be uniform) by observing frequencies in data generated from a chance process. For example, find the approximate probability that a spinning penny will land heads up or that a tossed paper cup will land open-end down. Do the outcomes for the spinning penny appear to be equally likely based on the observed frequencies?

NAME:

SCORE:

DATA BEING GRAPHED:

CHANCE OF EVENT A:

CHANCE OF EVENT B:

CHANCE OF BOTH EVENTS A & B:

GRAPH/TABLE OF RESULTS:

REFLECTIONS ABOUT DATA:

_____

_____

_____

7.SP.C.8.A: *Find probabilities of compound events using organized lists, tables, tree diagrams, and simulation.Understand that, just as with simple events, the probability of a compound event is the fraction of outcomes in the sample space for which the compound event occurs.*

GRADE 7 WORKSHEETS: 7.SP.C.8.B-C

NAME:

SCORE:

DATA BEING GRAPHED:

CHANCE OF EVENT A:

GRAPH/TABLE OF RESULTS:

CHANCE OF EVENT B:

CHANCE OF BOTH EVENTS A & B:

HOW ARE THE OUTCOMES TESTED?

REFLECTIONS ABOUT DATA ACCURACY:

7.SP.C.8.B: *Represent sample spaces for compound events using methods such as organized lists, tables and tree diagrams. For an event described in everyday language (e.g., "rolling double sixes"), identify the outcomes in the sample space which compose the event.*

7.SP.C.8.B: *Design and use a simulation to generate frequencies for compound events. For example, use random digits as a simulation tool to approximate the answer to the question: If 40% of donors have type A blood, what is the probability that it will take at least 4 donors to find one with type A blood?*

ABOUT THE AUTHOR

Andrew Frinkle is an award-nominated teacher and writer with experience in America and overseas. He has taught PreK all the way up to adult classes, and has focused on ESOL and EFL techniques. With a young child at home now, he's been developing more and more teaching strategies and books aimed at helping young learners.

His many educational works include:

• 50 STEM Labs & 50 More STEM Labs

• Common Core Assessment Templates

• Common Core Vocabulary Cards

• Graph Paper Math

• How to Draw with Basic Shapes

• Science Now!

• Sentence Builders & Word Builders

• Weekly Sentence Strips

• Story Starters

• Movers and Shakers & the Expansion Sets

• Basic Skills Workbooks: Alphabet Skills, Number Sense, and Shapes

• Monster Zoo Math

• Dealing With Archetypical Children - A Classroom Management Resource

• How to Draw Comic Books

• *Get this and other books on Amazon, Lulu, and other online booksellers!*

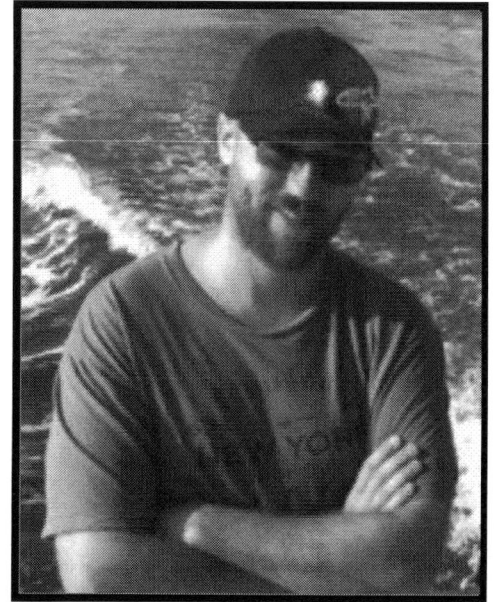

Read more about Andrew Frinkle at www.underspace.org. He also maintains the educational websites www.littlelearninglabs.com and www.common-core-assessments.com. He also works full time for www.havefunteaching.com and its affiliated sites, as well as writing fantasy and science fiction novels under the pen name Velerion Damarke.

Made in the USA
Middletown, DE
12 August 2020